PRAYERS AND MIRACLES

From Glory To Glory

ESTELLA HOLIDAY

outskirts
press

To My Prayer Partners:
Prayers and Miracles is a continuation of the first
book entitled Prayers that Touch God's Heart.

This volume is dedicated to:
the Father, the Son, and the Holy Spirit.

Forward March

When it comes to God and the gifts he has assigned to my hands, his thoughts and recommendations are always higher than my thoughts and plans.

I wanted to publish the next book about my personal life experiences growing up in Georgia and New Jersey, but the Holy Spirit said there were more prayers that needed to be shared with the body of Christ. This time, I also included some of the wonderful miracles that God has performed in my life because of his love for me.

Today more than ever we need to pray and share the great miracles that God has performed in our lives.

Our heavenly Father knows what's best for us, and I know he is proud of this book, entitled Prayers and Miracles, because it will inspire and encourage his children to talk to him and allow him to take them from glory to glory in their personal prayer lives.

The blessings of God overtake you, in the name of Jesus, forever!

TABLE OF CONTENTS

SECTION ONE
PRAYERS FROM THE HEART

LORD, SAVE MY CHILDREN

Mark 10:14-16

Father God,

Jesus was so displeased with his disciples when they tried to stop young children from approaching him to receive their blessings.

Your word says that children are a gift of your love to us. They are the crown of old men, and children receive their glory from their fathers. You commanded children to obey and honor their parents in the Lord because it pleases you, and it brings them promises of well-being and long life on the earth.

Jesus, I accepted you as my Lord and Savior very late in life, but I did not raise my children by biblical standards, and your name was rarely mentioned in my household.

My adult children are not teaching my grandchildren about Jesus, and God's love and plan of salvation for this world. When I mention the name of Jesus, my children rebuke me, and refuse to talk about him in their homes.

Lord, this grieves my heart and I feel like a failure. I want to see all my children in heaven with me one day. My children are wealthy in the things of this world, but they are spiritually dead, and wiser in their generation than your children of light.

Father God, you have not given up on this sinful world, and I will not give up on my children. I will continue to pray for them and walk in faith. I believe that you will reach them by your Holy Spirit and give each child an opportunity to receive Jesus as Lord and Savior.

Father, I come before you today with a humble heart asking you to save my children and bless them with your seal of salvation for generations to come, in the name of Jesus.

GOD, FORGIVE MY DIVORCE

Mark 10:4-12

Father God,

From the beginning when you created male and female and joined them in marriage, divorce was not part of the marriage covenant, but Moses allowed it because of the hardness of our hearts.

Father God, I believe it hurts your heart to see the divorce rate among your blood-brought children as high as the divorce rate for the children of disobedience.

We have failed to honor you in our marriage vows, and we have allowed the world to convince us that it's "OK" to be unfaithful and commit adultery against each other. We are being destroyed for the lack of knowledge and understanding of what it means to become one flesh in marriage. We are poor examples to unbelievers who feel that marriage is not for them, and they prefer to live together outside of a marriage covenant.

Jesus, I am a product of divorce because I did not follow your instructions in your Holy Word, and my marriage ended in bitterness, hurt, and shame. I ask that you forgive me for disobeying your guidelines for a Godly marriage.

Father, I pray now, in the name of Jesus, for all my brothers and sisters who have given up on their marriages and are facing divorce. Let your Spirit of Reconciliation overtake them with a fresh anointing to fight for their marriages. Restore their love for each other with meekness, kindness, and a tender heart to forgive one another for the sake of Christ.

MY HUSBAND IS BLESSED

Genesis 1:26-28

Father God,

I acknowledge you as my creator, and my spiritual husband who is the God of the whole earth. Thank you for blessing me with a man created after your own heart, who found me worthy to become his wife.

My husband is blessed because you made him in your image and in your likeness, and you gave him dominion over the works of your hands. Now teach him how to love you with all his heart and with all his soul, and to obey your voice.

Father, thank you for making my husband fruitful in his work and fruitful in his body. Our children, and all those who know him, respect him as a man of God because of your anointing on his life. Jesus, you are the life support in our marriage, and we depend on your love and guidance to keep us together.

My husband and I face challenges every day, and we have learned to lean and depend on your Holy Word as our shield to block the fiery darts of the devil. Thank you, Lord Jesus!

My husband has learned to trust me with his heart, and his needs. Father, strengthen me daily to always be there for him, especially in the areas of his life where he needs me the most.

Father God, your word says that our bodies are not our own, but are the temples of your Holy Spirit, which you have joined together in a marriage covenant. I do not seek to be loosed from my husband, and I promise to love him like Christ loved the Church and laid down his life for his bride.

MY WIFE IS BLESSED

Proverbs 18:22

Father God,

I believe I have found a good wife and she is blessed with your favor. Thank you for helping me find my mate. She is a beautiful person, and I am pleased to call her my wife. She is blessed with your wisdom and your knowledge. She knows how to maintain our home with peace and with love.

My wife is my crown and she is full of your virtue, Father God. She knows how to calm me down when I open the door for the spirit of pride, or the spirit of anger to come against me. I see your integrity in her heart when she conducts the business affairs of our household. She is a gracious woman full of your honor. My wife is a praying woman who respects me and allows me to be the priest over our home.

My love for my wife is priceless, and I believe I can trust her with all my heart for the rest of my days. She works willingly with her hands to keep our children and myself happy and secure. She rises early in the mornings to ensure that food is prepared for our family. My wife wants the best for us, and she also has a concern for the poor and the needy.

Father, I ask for your continued blessings upon my wife. Strengthen her in every area of her life. You gave me a beautiful woman full of your wisdom and kindness. She knows how to love me and love our kids. Praising her and showing appreciation for her is so easy and joyful for me and the children.

My wife loves you, Jesus, with all her heart; that's

why I love her with all my heart. Let her enjoy the fruit of her labor, the gifts of her hands, and let her walk in divine health even as her soul prospers all the days of her life, in the name of Jesus.

DELIVERED FROM FORNICATION

1 Corinthians 6:18-20

Father God,

You commanded in your word for us to flee from fornication because it is a sin against our bodies. We are the temples of your Holy Spirit, and our bodies belong to you.

Father, you also commanded us *not to be* deceived. Fornicators will not inherit your kingdom. You want us to have our own husband, or our own wife, and not allow fornication to destroy our marriages. It is better for us to marry than to burn with lust.

When I sinned against your word and violated your marriage covenant, you never gave up on me and accepted me back into your royal family. I am now joined to Jesus through the Holy Spirit.

Jesus, your blood has washed me, sanctified me, and justified me as the righteous of God. You never left me alone to fend for myself.

I depend on you daily, Father God, to help me raise my child according to your holy standards. I believe in my heart that you have blessed my child with your divine favor and surrounded him with your love and protection. When he fully understands your plan of salvation, Father, I pray in the name of Jesus that he will confess Christ as his personal Lord and Savior and give his life to you.

PRAY AGAINST CANCER

Matthew 18:18-20

Father God,

Jesus said in Matthew 18, "If two people will touch and agree on earth, anything that they ask, it shall be done for them by my Father in heaven."

My family and I are gathered in your name, Jesus, and we know you are with us in the Holy Spirit.

We received a negative report from the doctor this week, but we will not be afraid of this evil report. We choose to believe your report, Lord Jesus. It says you were wounded for our transgressions, our sickness, and our diseases. You were chastised for our peace. Your bloody stripes have healed every form of cancer that afflicts mankind — past, present, and future. The sin and iniquity of all men were laid upon you on the cross.

Jesus, you have already redeemed my brother from the law, and the curse of cancer, when you died on the cross for him. By faith, my brother has received your promise of healing from cancer in your new covenant of grace.

Today, according to your word, Father, we bind the cancer spirit called *carcinoid* in my brother's body, and we loose the healing stripes in your blood, Jesus, to kill and dry up every tumor mass that has invaded and covered every organ in his body. *Carcinoid*, we render you powerless by the authority and in the name of Jesus, and we command you to go now from my brother's body.

Thank you for the life and the power in your word, Father God. By your Holy Spirit, we believe your healing power has been released in my brother's body. The world will see that the name of Jesus is greater, and more powerful, than the spirit of cancer and the works of the devil. Cancer must bow to your holy name, Jesus.

RESPECT GOD'S AUTHORITY

Romans 13:1

Father God,

You ordained the higher powers that exist on earth today for our protection and our good. The powers were created for the lawless and designed to execute punishment against evil in the land.

Father, you told us to show love and pray for those who persecute and curse us. You commanded us to be honest in our dealings with everyone, overcome evil with good, and obey and respect the laws of the earth.

You are calling us this day to humble ourselves, turn from evil, and pray if we desire to see crime and drug-infected neighborhoods healed, see the hand of God war against gun violence in our schools, and see a sharp decrease of spiritual wickedness in the high places of our government.

Lord, help us to cast off the works of darkness, rioting, drunkenness, strife, and envying. Give us your supernatural strength to walk in the armor of your light with love.

Father God, I pray that the spirit of honor and respect for your authority will overtake your children on the earth. I believe by faith that the body of Christ will hear and obey your voice to repent, turn from evil, and honor the powers and authorities you gave us for our good, in the name of Jesus.

DISCIPLESHIP IN JESUS

Luke 9:59-62

Father God,

In the book of Luke, Jesus said, "No man, having put his hand to the plow, and looking back, is fit for the kingdom of God."

There have been times in my life when I did not deny myself, take up my cross daily, and follow Jesus. My personal agenda became my priority.

When you told me to go and show kindness to my neighbors, I made up excuses for not following your instructions. I was just too busy doing my own thing.

Father God, thank you for giving me time to repent and turn my life around. As I mature in your Holy Word, I understand now that you must be first in my life before my family, friends, and my job.

My heart's desire is to be your disciple, and not just a believer in your salvation. I want to bear my cross and follow you, Jesus, regardless of what happens in my life.

Father, I want to be a person after your own heart, who will go after the lost sheep until he has been found, then rejoice over his salvation with your angels in heaven. I want to be seasoned salt in your kingdom.

Jesus, help me to get out of my comfort zone and spend quality time with you in prayer and fasting, and boldly use the power and authority you gave me to proclaim the good news of your gospel, heal the sick, cast out demons, and raise the dead in your matchless and holy name.

MEMBERS HAVE EARS

1 Corinthians 12:14-26

Father God,

When you designed the human body to be the dwelling place for our spirits and souls on the earth, you created the body with many members, as it pleased you. You gave each member a specific function to avoid division in the body.

The hand cannot say to the foot, "I don't need you," nor can the ear dislike the eye, because they need each other to support the body.

Many are the afflictions of the righteous, but Jesus has delivered us from all of them. He has provided help for us when our bodies are under attack by the enemy.

Jesus, thank you for providing me with a medical team that ministers to my physical body, and prescribes medicines to help my body carry out its divine purpose.

Holy Spirit, thank you for reminding me to pray for my medical team, which God has placed in my life. Remind me to speak the blessings of God over my medications before I take them.

Jesus, I know that healing is my daily bread, and it comes from you. My body is the temple of your Holy Spirit. Death and life are in the power of my tongue.

You gave me authority over my physical body to speak those things that are not as though they are, by faith in your name.

Therefore, I will speak healing to the members in my body, and they will hear me and obey my voice, in the name of Jesus.

NOT ASHAMED OF JESUS

Luke 9:26

Father God,

There have been times in my life when I should have stood firmly and defended the name of Jesus in conversations with unbelievers, but I was intimidated by their words and kept silent.

Father God, I repent, and I ask you to forgive me for being ashamed of your son, Jesus Christ. I receive your forgiveness with a grateful heart. Thank you for forgiving me and loving me in spite of my sins.

Your Holy Spirit is teaching me how to understand and speak the truth of your word. It has life, power, and authority to save the lost. I will not be ashamed of the gospel of Jesus Christ from this day forward.

Lord, you can trust me and send me forth as a lamb among wolves because your Holy Spirit has control of my life. I will suffer persecution for the sake of Christ and I will not be ashamed.

I will endure hardships as a good soldier of Jesus Christ. I will be satisfied and not be complaining in times of famine.

The times are evil on the earth, but your word, Father, will hold me up and I will not be ashamed of Jesus, my hope of glory. I trust in you and I will not be ashamed and afraid to speak to my enemies and they will not triumph over me, in the name of Jesus.

THE GOD OF SECRETS
AND DREAMS

Daniel 2:9-10

Father God,

Blessed is your holy name forever and ever because true wisdom, understanding, and interpretation of dreams and secrets of the heart comes from you.

Astrologers, magicians, and sorcerers of this worldly system are false prophets with familiar spirits and should not have access to secrets hidden in the hearts of the children of God. These secrets belong to you, Father, and to the remnant you have called by your holy name.

Your sons and daughters prophesy, old men dream dreams, and your young men see visions by the Holy Spirit.

Father God, you have shown the world your signs and wonders in the heavens and the earth with pillars of fire and smoke, and the moon became blood. But the world still rejects your wisdom, knowledge, and understanding, and continues in its wickedness and sorcery with the workers of witchcraft sent by the powers of evil.

Lord, remind us again by your Spirit that psychic phone networks and witchcraft are tools of the devil designed to fulfill the lustful desires of our flesh. These devices do not bring honor and glory to your holy name.

I pray in the name of Jesus that your children will flee from the works of the devil and seek you for the answers to all their dreams, and the deep secrets of their hearts.

PLEAD THE BLOOD
OF JESUS

Exodus 12:13

Father God,

When you passed over Egypt to smite all the firstborn in the land, the blood of a lamb (type and shadow of Jesus) protected your children from the plague.

Therefore, I plead the blood of Jesus over my children, grandchildren, friends, and siblings to protect them from gun violence on the streets, in schools, on jobs, in churches, and from contagious germs, medical mistakes, diseases, and infected people with deadly diseases.

The blood of Jesus protects my natural and spiritual family from violent sexual acts and from being kidnapped against their will, in the name of Jesus.

I plead the blood of Jesus over my global brothers and sisters in the body of Christ who travel the world to spread the gospel of Jesus Christ. The blood of Jesus prevails against religious scribes and Pharisees who try to prevent the preaching of God's word worldwide.

I plead the blood of Jesus over my property and my home to protect against acts of violence by evildoers. Before I go on vacation or travel in my neighborhood, I plead the blood of Jesus. My finances are under the blood of Jesus to protect against the thieves and robbers of this world.

I will plead the blood of Jesus all my life over every situation. The devil will flee from me and he must bow to the name of Jesus. Father God, thank you for the blood of Jesus!

ONE NATION UNDER GOD

Psalm 33:12

Father God,

By your Holy Spirit, you sent the pilgrims from across the world to settle in America to worship your holy name. The words "In God We Trust" were engraved (by our forefathers) in the monetary and judicial systems of our nation to honor and acknowledge your blessings upon this land.

Father, you blessed us with a land flowing with milk and honey. You told us to be fruitful, multiply, populate the land, and dominate it, but use the resources to honor and glorify your holy name. You made America a great nation to serve as an example to other nations around the world.

Your word says blessed is the nation who has chosen God as Lord of their righteousness, but sin is a disgrace to any nation. A righteous nation that upholds the truth of God and trusts in him will be victorious in the presence of their enemies because Jesus is their Lord.

Father, we have disobeyed you and lost respect for your Holy Word, rejected your corrections, called your truth a lie, and called a lie your truth. We are a rebellious nation that has transgressed against you in every way. You have sent us warning after warning and we have yet to repent as a nation and ask for your forgiveness. The body of Christ is not united in love as we should be, and the world no longer respects us.

Jesus, you died for our nation, and we need your help to regain our respect as the body of Christ. Strengthen us to stand strong with one voice and declare in faith and in the name of Jesus that we are one nation under God, the Father, once again. Amen.

BLESSED NOT STRESSED

Proverbs 10:22

Father God,

Your word says your blessings for me are rich without sorrow, and your thoughts of me are not evil, but thoughts of peace. I am blessed to be a vessel of your glory.

You have blessed my bread and my water and taken sickness out of my body. You have given me your peace to satisfy my soul. My life has been redeemed from destruction and crowned with your love, tender mercies, and kindness, and I am filled with your goodness.

Even though I came from the dust of the earth, you have renewed my youth like the eagle. Father, I will honor your name continuously and songs of praise will always be in my mouth.

I will stand and bless your glorious name every day and worship you in the beauty of holiness. You have saved me from hell and blessed me with your gift of eternal life.

You have surrounded me with your shield of favor and made Jesus the portion of my inheritance and the rock of my salvation.

Blessed is your name, Father God, forevermore, in the name of Jesus. Amen.

JEREMIAH FIRE

Jeremiah 20:9

Father God,

Your word is in my heart like a burning fire shut up in my bones, and I cannot keep silent about your goodness and your mercy from this day forward.

Father, I will go where you send me and speak what you have commanded me to say. Even though the world will fight against me, I will not be afraid of their faces because you are with me to deliver and protect me and the devil will not prevail against me.

I will use your authority to pull down and destroy the works of evil in the name of Jesus in the nations and kingdoms of this world. I will speak loudly against the wickedness that has polluted our lands and caused great suffering among the people on the earth.

I will plead with those who have forsaken you, Father, and turned to other gods for help, and worshipped idols made by their own hands. I will plead with them to return to the God of our salvation, Jesus Christ.

Father, I repent of all my sins and stand in the spirit of repentance on behalf of our nation. Jesus, forgive us of all our sins, and help us to return to you, because you are our fountain of living waters, and only you can bring healing to our nation. In the name of Jesus, I pray.

THE HOLY GHOST: OUR COMFORTER

John 14:16-17,26

Father God,

Thank you for giving us the Holy Ghost. He is your promise and comforter, who came down to earth from your kingdom in heaven. You sent him in the name of Jesus to teach us all things and bring all things to our remembrance according to your Holy Word.

The Holy Ghost is your Spirit of truth, and only your righteous seed, Father, can see him and know him, because he dwells in us and is with us forever. Your love lives and shines through us because of the Holy Ghost. His voice will only speak what's in your heart because he knows your mind and your thoughts.

Father, we are so blessed because you ordained the Holy Ghost to be the teacher and overseer of the body of Christ before the foundation of the world. He is our eternal witness that Jesus purchased us with his own blood.

Thank you for using the Holy Ghost to warn us against unforeseen dangers and ungodly advice spoken by evildoers. He is the spiritual pathway into your presence, Father God. He has helped me to resist rebellion, be truthful, and told me not to grieve your Spirit through disobedience. The Holy Ghost became my intercessor in prayer when I did not know how to pray, and what to pray for. He sent me to the right body of believers, so I can grow in your Holy Word.

Thank you, Father God, for your gift of love, the Holy Ghost, who all can receive when Jesus has become their Lord and Savior. You have baptized me with the Holy Ghost, your divine power, wisdom, and faith, to do good works and heal all oppressed by the devil. I am forever grateful to you, in the name of Jesus.

OUR TEARS MATTER

Psalm 126:5, 56:8

Father God,

It is my desire to always walk before you in truth with a perfect heart and do what is pleasing in your sight. I know that you hear my prayers and collect my tears. Our nation is in trouble and we need your deliverance, Father.

I see the evil and destructive weather patterns that have come upon the people of this earth. Families are crying, weeping, and wailing in the streets over the death of their children, taken through violent acts of crime and authorities controlled by the evil one.

I am exceedingly grieved, and I cannot hold my peace any longer. I come before your throne of grace, Father, in tears, asking for mercy and the abundance of grace to help us in a time of great need.

I pray in the name of Jesus for the righteous remnant of Christ to rise and cry loud against injustice in the Holy Spirit, and to not keep silent. You are waiting for us to seek your heart and your righteousness, to break the chains of affliction that have infected our land. Lord, let our tears flow like deep waters upon your altar. Your word says they that sow in tears shall reap joy.

Thank you, Father God, for sending your angels to collect all the tears to fill your bottles in heaven. Blessed is the God of our salvation forever! Amen.

I AM NOT OF THIS WORLD

1 Chronicles 29:15

Father God,

You know my end from my beginning and the measure of my days are like a shadow to you. My age is only a second in your sight, and I am a pilgrim in this world created from the dust of the earth. When I return to the dust, you will keep my soul alive and I will dwell in your house forever in a place of honor.

You took me out of my mother's womb and gave me hope as I lay upon her breasts. Jesus has delivered me from the oppressions of my enemies and made me the head and not the tail. Strangers do honor me and serve me with gladness. Only Jesus Christ will have dominion over my life.

I am your seed and you have blessed me to eat and be satisfied with the fruit of my labor. Thank you, Father, for putting the devil under your feet in the earth; he must come through you to get to me. To God be the glory, in the name of Jesus! Amen.

THE LORD OF THE HARVEST

Matthew 9:37-38

Father God,

Help us to be moved with greater compassion for those who are weak and scattered abroad like sheep without a shepherd. Remind us again that our time on earth is short and Jesus is coming soon. In the book of Matthew, Jesus said whoever does the will of my Father in heaven is my brother, my sister, and my mother. I rebuke the spirit of division and envy between the male and the female over positions of power and authority in the church, and I pray for a spirit of oneness to overtake the body of Christ.

We must fulfill your great commission to go into the world and preach the gospel of Jesus Christ to everyone and baptize all believers in the name of Jesus. Father, I pray that we crucify self and allow the Holy Spirit to work signs and wonders through us, giving you the glory and the honor due your name.

Father, you are the Lord of the harvest for the earth. I pray in the name of Jesus that you will send forth more laborers full of your Holy Spirit into your harvest to reap souls for your kingdom. Your fields are ripe and ready for harvest and your souls will not perish and shall be gathered before the end of the world according to your divine purpose. In the name of Jesus, I pray. Amen.

JESUS IS WILLING TO HEAL

Matthew 8:3

Father God,

I thank you that Jesus is still in the healing business, and he is willing to heal us today from all manner of sickness and disease that attack our physical bodies. Jesus lived a sinless life among the people on the earth and obeyed the voice of your Holy Spirit.

When the leper came and worshipped Jesus, immediately he was healed. The centurion recognized and believed in the power and authority of words spoken by Jesus, and his servant was healed that same hour. Peter's mother-in-law lay sick with a fever, but when Jesus touched her hand, the fever left immediately.

He healed a man with palsy and forgave his sins. Jesus raised a child from the dead and released healing into the body of the woman with the issue of blood because she touched him in faith. Two blind men received their sight because they believed that Jesus could heal them. He called a heathen woman a dog, but she did not get offended and received the crumbs from the healing table of heaven.

Father, you suffered Jesus's back to be ripped open with thirty-nine blood-filled stripes that bared all the infirmities, sicknesses, and diseases of the earth, so that mankind through him could be healed and made whole in the name of Jesus. Thank you, Father God. Amen.

GOD OF RESTORATION

Joel 2:25

Father God,

I know that it is your heart's desire to restore the years that the locust has stolen from me. You do not want me to be a reproach among the rebellious on the earth.

Therefore, I will return to you with all my heart with fasting, weeping, and mourning. I will look to you my Lord and my God because you are gracious, merciful, slow to anger, and rich in kindness.

I will not fear but stand in faith, and you will deliver me from my enemies. I will be glad and rejoice for the great blessings that you will rain down from the windows of heaven upon me.

I will be satisfied and praise your name forever, Father God. You are my hope and the strength of my salvation in the name of Jesus. Amen.

THE EFFECTS OF
GOD'S WORD

Hebrews 4:12

Father God,

You do not speak to us with a double heart or with flattering lips and your words are pure. Every word that comes out of your mouth is perfect, true and righteous. Abraham believed your word and became the father of faith to generations of believers in Christ. You sent your word and King Hezekiah was delivered from death's door and received fifteen more years of life. The Virgin Mary by the Holy Ghost gave birth to your son, Jesus, because she had faith and believed your word.

Your word is sharper than any two-edged sword. It is life and power to those who believe it and speak it in faith. It is health to my joints and marrow and a judge of the thoughts and intents of my heart.

Your word has humbled me and restored my soul to peace. I cried to you in the time of trouble and your word brought me out of my distress. It calmed the storms and commanded the waves to be still.

Father, your word is my strength, my joy, and my salvation. It will stand forever in the name of Jesus. Amen.

SECTION TWO
A LIFE OF MIRACLES

Today, more than ever, we need to let the world know that our heavenly Father not only answers prayer, but he is a miracle-working God. I was inspired by the Holy Spirit to share some of the miracles that have taken place in my life over the years.

My first miracle took place when my son was five years old and I was in my second year of college. My mother came to New Jersey to spend time with her grandchildren. When she came to visit me, there was very little food left in my refrigerator and I had run out of money and was too embarrassed to tell my mother. The devil told me to go out on the street corner and I could make some quick money.

Instead, I went to class that night and on my way home a drunk man got on the bus two blocks before my stop. There were plenty of seats and a few people still left on the bus. The man passed all those empty seats and sat next to me. He forcefully put the money in my hand. I tried to give it back, but he would not take it. Then someone yelled, "Lady, if you don't take that money, I'll take it!" I took the money.

The man got off the bus at the next stop in front of a bar and went in. I got off the bus at the next stop and ran home as fast as I could to count that money. It was seventy-eight dollars. I had seventy-eight cents in my pocket when the angel of God got on my bus that night.

My next miracle occurred when my son turned seven years old and I needed to go to my local bank to withdraw money. I completed the transaction, walked out of the bank with my money, and left my purse on the counter. I suddenly realized that I did not have my purse in my hand. When I returned to the bank it was gone and there were no witnesses to the theft. I was so hurt. The thought of losing and having to replace all my personal documents would take some time. Less than a week later I received a brown bag in the mail that contained my purse with all my documents intact. The only thing missing was eight dollars that had been in the purse before it was stolen.

A year later my mother passed away in Georgia, and when I returned to New Jersey after her funeral I had car trouble and had to leave my vehicle in Newark at a local garage in the area and take the bus home. The next day I went to the garage to check on my car, but the man who promised to fix the mechanical issue was not there and my car was gone. The mechanics at the garage said they did not know the man and could not recall what happened to my vehicle. I was dumbstruck.

I returned home, called the police, and reported the car stolen. The Holy Spirit of God told me I would get my car back. Six months after I bought a new car, I got a phone call from a young man that had bought my stolen vehicle from another guy. The young man asked me for the title because he found out that I was the real owner. He came to my home with his mother and I explained to him that the car had been stolen from me months earlier. I sold the car to them for six hundred dollars and signed the title. I immediately called the police and had the car removed from the stolen car list.

In 1989, a door opened for me to interview and possibly work for one of the largest banks in New Jersey. I said to God, "If you bless me to get this position, I will give you ten percent of the gross (3,400 dollars) first year salary as tithe." Well, I got the job, then the Holy Spirit reminded me of my vow to the Lord. I went to the bank and withdrew the money, then I asked God what he wanted me to do with it. He told me to give it to my pastor. I obeyed God and my pastor told me later the 3,400 dollars is what he had believed God for to pay off his hospital bill.

In 1996, my bank was bought out by a larger bank and I was laid off from my job, but God opened a position for me to work for a transportation and logistics company. I accepted the job, but the starting salary was seven thousand dollars below the old job salary at the bank. God restored that pay cut two years later through a human resources job industry upgrade.

In 2003, I went to lunch at a local mall down the street from my office. I was loaded down with shopping bags and leftover lunch when I returned to my car. I dropped my purse in the parking space where my car was parked outside the mall, got into my car, and went back to work, parked the car, finished off my lunch, and took a nap in the car. Almost two hours later, I could not find my purse, and I panicked! The Holy Spirit told me to calm down and go back to the mall to the place where I had parked. When I arrived at the mall, the area only had one car parked directly in front of my previous parking spot, and a man was sitting in that car eating lunch, but he never looked up at me. My purse was lying there in the spot where I dropped it, totally exposed to the public. I picked it up and praised God for protecting my personal items. The Holy Spirit said to me that the blood of Jesus not only protects me, but everything that belongs to me.

In November of 2008, huge red lumps broke out on my face, suddenly, overnight without warning. I went to my primary doctor, but the lotions he prescribed had no effect on my facial condition. I complained to the Lord, but the Holy Ghost reminded me that I am healed now, and should use my health insurance to treat the physical effects of the skin condition. I went to a skin specialist and a skin biopsy was taken for lab processing. The results revealed that I had been attacked by a foreign, unidentified infectious strain that caused my immune system to fight against itself. The doctor called it dense sarcoidosis in the facial skin. For the next two years, I spoke healing over my condition and followed the doctor's orders until the physical healing manifestation was completed. To God be the glory!

In November 2010, I was driving home on a Friday night after work. I had my gospel music on and I was having a wonderful time singing and praising the Lord. Suddenly, two huge brown deer ran across the four-lane highway. The first deer made it past my car, but the second deer literally passed through the front of my car and kept on running. I was so amazed! I asked God, "Lord, what just happened here?" I heard the Holy Spirit say, "You just experienced traveling mercies." That Friday morning before I left home for work, I specifically prayed for traveling mercies to cover me that day. I shared my miracle with my Bible study group at church. The group leader told me that same miracle had happened to our pastor's wife as she was on her way home earlier in the month.

In December of 2013, there was a combined snow and ice storm in northern New Jersey, and I wanted to get to work early one morning so I could leave work early. The local road was only two lanes, with no sidewalks and several curves before the entrance to the main street. I was driving too fast that morning and the road had been poorly plowed. I lost control of my vehicle when I hit a patch of ice and was headed toward the telephone pole on the side of the road. I yelled "Jesus!" as loud as I could and immediately an invisible hand began to turn my car back into the road and I barely missed the pole. I looked in my car mirror and the cars behind me had stopped, expecting me to hit the pole head on, but it didn't happen. The Holy Spirit helped me regained my composure and control of my car and I kept on driving. To God be the glory!

My sister and I were driving home on May 28, 2018, after visiting my grandchildren in Florida. We checked out of the hotel at 4:30 a.m. and a nail had punctured the rear tire on the driver side. The tire pressure signal did not display until I was on the interstate driving seventy-five miles an hour. My sister checked the manual to confirm that it was indeed a tire pressure problem. I was really concerned and got off at the next available exit. When I pulled into the local gas station and drove to the air machine, my back tire immediately lost air pressure and the machine was not working. There were several men standing at the machine conversing. One of the men asked me if I had a spare, and I said no. I had nothing but a flat tire. He immediately went into the store and purchased a can of sealant for me and told me to park the car to the side of the station away from incoming traffic. Then he told me that he was going to get something to plug the hole in the tire before applying the sealant. The man returned within fifteen minutes with everything he needed to fix my tire and get us back on the road. His name was Thomas. He never asked for any money and said that he was very happy to be able to help us get home. I told Thomas that he was ordained by God to be there at the right time for us. We gave him forty dollars and an autographed copy of my prayer book, *Prayers that Touch God's Heart*. After we got back on the road, my sister told me that while she was sleeping earlier that morning she had a dream that we had a flat tire and was afraid to tell me because I might think she was crazy. No, I think the spirit of panic would have taken hold of me and affected my thought process and the Holy Spirit knew how I would react. He already had a perfect plan in place to deliver us from trouble.

God has performed numerous miracles in my life, but these are just some of the miracles that I recorded and never wanted to forget. I am so happy that Jesus chose me to be a part of his eternal kingdom. It is my prayer that someone will be blessed and inspired after reading my testimonies and believe that God is still working miracles today. Just believe God, no matter what the circumstances are right now. God's best is yet to come for you.

Bible Resource

King James Version Holy Bible: Giant Print

Thomas Nelson, Publisher 1976

Nashville, Tennessee 37214

Appendix

My prayers were adapted from the following scriptures:

Lord, Save My Children:	Mark 10:14-16
God, Forgive My Divorce	Mark 10:4-12
My Husband Is Blessed	Genesis 1:26-28
My Wife Is Blessed	Proverbs 18:22
Delivered from Fornication	1 Corinthians 6:18-20
Pray against Cancer 18:18-20	Matthew
Respect God's Authority	Romans 13:1
Discipleship in Jesus	Luke 9:59-62
Members Have Ears 12:14-26	1 Corinthians
Not Ashamed of Jesus	Luke 9:26
The God of Secrets and Dreams	Daniel 2:9-10
Plead the Blood of Jesus	Exodus 12:13
One Nation under God	Psalm 33:12
Blessed Not Stressed	Proverbs 10:22
Jeremiah Fire	Jeremiah 20:9

The Holy Ghost:	John 14:16-17,26
Our Comforter	
Our Tears Matter	Psalm 126:5, 56:8
I Am Not of This World	1 Chronicles 29:15
The Lord of the Harvest	Matthew 9:37-38
Jesus Is Willing to Heal	Matthew 8:3
God of Restoration	Joel 2:25
The Effects of God's Word	Hebrews 4:12

CPSIA information can be obtained
at www.ICGtesting.com
Printed in the USA
FSHW012005310821
84446FS